OWLING

OWLING

poems by Jeredith Merrin

GRAYSON BOOKS
WEST HARTFORD, CT
www.GraysonBooks.com

OWLING
Copyright © 2016, Jeredith Merrin
Published by Grayson Books
West Hartford, Connecticut
Printed in the USA

ISBN: 978-0-9962809-7-6

Book & Cover Design: Cindy Mercier
Cover Art: Eurasian Eagle Owl, color lithograph by Edward Lear, courtesy of Age Fotostock America Inc.

GraysonBooks.com

For Diane Furtney

"When we try to pick out anything by itself, we find it hitched to everything else in the Universe."

—John Muir

Acknowledgments

Able Muse Review　　　The Burrowing Owl
　　　　　　　　　　　　The Pharaoh Eagle Owl

Berfrois　　　　　　　　The Barn Owl
　　　　　　　　　　　　The Barn Owl (2)
　　　　　　　　　　　　The Elf Owl
　　　　　　　　　　　　The Flammulated Owl

Fiddlehead　　　　　　　The Great Gray Owl
　　　　　　　　　　　　The Snowy Owl (earlier version)

Zoomorphic　　　　　　 The Maned Owl

My thanks to Vivian Shipley for selecting my little parliament of owls and to Ginny Connors for her kindliness and editorial expertise. Gratitude to poets Jim Powell, Mark Doty, and Alan Shapiro for useful feedback and encouragement. To the Hive poetry group in Phoenix and to Changing Hands Bookstore's Poetry Roundtable, merci. Special thanks to Helen Deutsch and Elizabeth Lockman for their friendship and support, and to Barbara Levy, Jon Ward, and Gay Hadley.

Contents

The Pharaoh Eagle Owl	11
The Barn Owl	12
The Barn Owl (2)	13
The Burrowing Owl	15
The Elf Owl	18
The Guatemalan Pygmy Owl	19
The Little Owl	20
The Flammulated Owl	21
The Great Gray Owl	22
The Maned Owl	23
The Stygian Owl	24
The Spectacled Owl	25
The Great Horned Owl	28
Blakiston's Fish Owl	30
The Eastern Screech Owl	32
The Long-Whiskered Owlet	33
The Snowy Owl	34
Hume's Tawny Owl	36
The Barred Owl	37
About the Author	38
Notes and References	39

The Pharaoh Eagle Owl
(Bubo ascalaphus)

Look how it looks as it's looking
from an outcrop of rock:

buff, bleached rose, apricot,
blotched with dark and light—

sandstone rock, sandstone bird.

It could be carved *in situ*, like the sphinx.

What riddle is it posing,
large desert bird with deep, orange eyes?

What secret are you keeping from yourself?

Fierce and monogamous, it has nested in the pyramids.

This is the owl of hidden-but-not-altogether;
this is the owl of figure-it-out.

By day, camouflaged in a crevice,
a hunter, tonight.

The Barn Owl
(Tyto alba)

Though it roosts in abandoned
factories or barn-lofts,
this mid-sized, widespread

owl with dramatic, white, heart-
shaped facial disc is not
a human emblem—

its characteristic call
a penetrating *shree*,
feeding on voles, mice,

the occasional small bird;
summer nights hunting from
sundown to dawn, low-

flying, hovering on long,
sound-absorptive wings. Still,
met, of a sudden

—pale mask floating in full dark—
you might well mistake it
for a heart in shock.

The Barn Owl (2)
(Tyto alba)

Two more things:
butterscotch (which I'll get back to),
and hovering, which is hard to do:

part of the wing must keep the bird vertical
with an up-and-down motion,
but part has to stay its flight
with a forward-and-back.

It's something like a human
treading water,

or thinking. . .

Hannah Arendt, a friend once told me,
had a cot where she lay
until a thought was thought
through. Her husband
would not disturb her
for any caller:
"Hannah's *thinking*," he would say.

I repeated this to my mother
who responded, "How selfish!
She should get up for her guests."

—And, though functional for a barn owl
(flight on pause to spot prey
or feed mice to nested young),
does our peculiar version
of effortful suspension
pay off, always, for us?

Still, I thought the story beautiful,
which is how a barn owl's neck smells—
a mix of butterscotch, so they say,
and freshly washed sheets.

Imagine! Not a Zen master
tended by his disciples,
but a woman,
a married woman, defended
to hover in thought.

The Burrowing Owl
(Athene cunicularia)

In and out of

>fashion
>health
>favor

>>or, in this case,
>>burrows—

>>these grassland and desert owls,
>>with legs like stilts:
>>standing, surveying
>>the flat land around them
>>for beetles, scorpions, and other food.

In and out of

>shape
>humor
>tune

>>Busy squatters inhabiting
>>abandoned holes of gopher,
>>ground squirrel, tortoise,
>>coyote, or fox;

>>also, the tunnels of prairie dogs
>>(more like prairie popcorn,
>>that time I saw a colony,
>>so quick and so many
>>popping everywhere up&out).

In and out of

    order
    danger
    control

        In breeding season the male
        sun-bleaches to buff
        from standing guard outside,
        while she stays cream and brown,
        keeping indoors with their young

        (clever owlets that scare intruders
        by hissing-rattling like snakes).

In and out of

    practice
    season
    focus

        Yellow-eyed, white-eyebrowed.

In and out of

    trouble
    luck
    love

        Endangered masters
        of exiting and entering—

like Marilyn in *The Misfits*,
up Clark Gable's makeshift
concrete-block steps and into
the half-built house in the desert,
then down again, and up, over
and over, exclaiming
(wholly given to the game):

"I can go in! And I can come out!"

How in their last movie
her ample body seems so fragile
as she goes break-your-heart
back and forth from happy to sad.

No one like her; but we do that, we all do.

Out of sorts. In heaven.
In a quandary. Out of time.

The Elf Owl
    (Micrathene whitneyi)

We love what we like
to think like
ourselves:

familiar round, flattish face
and large, front-fac-
ing eyes

on a bird small
enough for a full-
sized owl's doll.

(This one would fit in
a zip-lock for check-in.)
Bewitched, you forgot

to note feathers—and razors!
The darling you fell for's
a raptor.

The Guatemalan Pygmy Owl
(Glaucidium cobanense)

The things we can't have:
my grandson—his boyhood dream-car, a Lamborghini. . .

And in *Owls of the World*, this one

—the same compact, cobby body,
orange-red, with cream patches—

in its rufous morph for all the world
like the creature I once coveted,
who batted a feather, enchanting the judges,
unaware of its own perfections,
oblivious to their decision:
"Best Kitten in Show."

The same tantalizing softness,
an avian version of the Persian-cat frown.

What we can't have,

and what we can't have back:

adolescent vigor, assumed to last forever;
the woods as they were, flush with tanagers, thrushes;
your own perfect newborn, pre-parental regrets.

To be is to be wanting:
a '56 Porthole T-Bird,
the National Book Award,
a deep understanding of double-disk dark matter,
this seven-inch, mountain-forest bird.
Feline ease—sturdy, cobby—with your life.

The Little Owl
(Athene noctua)

Low-browed, flat-headed, this six-ounce owl
inspires little faith in the size of its brain—
an unlikely emblem for the goddess of wisdom:

Athena Glaukopis, the gleaming-eyed, clear-eyed,
her city's coins stamped with the bird's likeness,
of Laurium silver; called *glaukes*, or owls.

> And Odysseus came home on the Phaeacian ship
> without knowing his country, not knowing Ithaca.
> Athena had covered the shore in a mist.
>
> "Whose land," he asks (in the Fagles translation),
> "have I lit on now? What *are* they here—
> violent, savage, lawless?—or friendly to strangers?"

It passes, his confusion, and he knows his own son—
unlike (long past that Bronze Age, in old age)
someone in my family, someone in your own.

> "Where have I come to? What *are* they, Glaukopis?"
> The island in thick mist, in fog.

The Flammulated Owl
(Psiloscops flammeolus)

Small owl with large, dark eyes—
like moth wings' hungry eyes,
which cannot, of course, see.

>We couldn't see what it would come to.

Ash-gray, mimicking bark
of Ponderosas, where it nests,
with flame-shaped, rust-red markings.

>A log in the fireplace, in childhood: remember?
>Worlds-within-worlds, glimmering, dimming
>to glimmer again. . .
>
>Possibility, aching—worlds, and words.

Ponderosa.

Insectivore. Nocturnal. Flammulated.

>O my grand, improbable passions. O yours.

The Great Gray Owl
(Strix nebulosa)

The German for the species is *bartkauz*
        or "bearded owl," which makes me think of a man
—maybe a father—whether bearded or not,
        with or without the wherewithal to love.

In North America, the largest owl
        in body length and length of wing; the largest
facial disk (marked by concentric rings,
        as in a cross-section of tree), the big head

fitted with a mottled hood, like bark.
        In air, it's like a flying, broken tree-stump,
and often, Grays will nest in broken trees,
        so seeing one flap out and up is startling,

like a blue whale breaching from blue water,
        or a blushing neediness erupting
from molten, subterranean, young-girl yearning. . .
        As it turns out, the bird's power is façade:

thick feathers make a smaller man look large—
        I mean a bird. I mean a man. How could
he give her what she couldn't keep from wanting?
        The owl, for all his feathers, was a-cold.

The Maned Owl
(Jubula lettii: classified in 2013 as "Data Deficient" by the *International Union for Conservation of Nature*)

About the maned owl
there is little to tell
because little is known.
It gets its leonine name
from bushy, face-framing
ear tufts. It lives
in Gambon, Cameroon,
Liberia, the Congo
(in what numbers we don't know),
in closed-canopy rainforest.
Its habits are secretive
and nocturnal. Presumably,
given heavy lumbering,
its survival's at risk.
About reproduction and diet,
information is scant.
Its call may be
(we're not sure)
a low, dove-like coo.
As is the case with
the wide coral reefs,
or with each creature's
closed-canopy mind,
or with almost anyone's
mother or father,
too little is known about them.
And then they're gone.

The Stygian Owl
(Asio stygius, a.k.a. *Coruja-diabo*)

Long, erect ear tufts, sooty
plumage, eyes glowing
red in the dark: enough
so that in Brazil
it's called "devil's owl;"
in the Caribbean,
linked to witchcraft,
it's killed. Unexamined
fear, projection, and
inimical naming—so helpful
for maintaining hate.
(When and where
have we seen *that* before?)
The bird's eye is backed
by the *tapetum lucidum*
or "bright tapestry,"
an iridescent tissue
that reflects light toward
the retina—the resulting
red gleam a common
feature of night hunters.
There is no Devil.

The Spectacled Owl
(Pulsatrix perspicillata)

Easier to socialize to the scrolleries of Mozart, I know—
so at the cocktail party the psychiatrist asked our hostess
to turn off the background Shostakovich: "disturbing."
But, as Darwin wrote, "Delight itself is a weak term
to express the feelings of a naturalist, who,
for the first time, has wandered by himself into
a Brazilian forest"—which was how we felt last week,
listening to Leonard Bernstein conduct un-easy
Dmitri's First. And this has *what* (you ask) to do with
a medium-to-large owl, fairly common in Brazil?

*

The unsociable bird's striking "spectacles" are formed
by white eyebrows and what are called "malar streaks and lores."
In his photo (1925), the composer's nineteen:
behind thick-lensed wire-rims, already isolate;
an almost girlish mouth, the clear refusal of a smile.
Compare him to the scowling owl, and you have to smile.

*

Easier, I know, to read a poem that begins:
"In love with my own male, suburban aloneness, I picked
up the paper from the driveway, slightly damp
in its plastic bag, neatly rolled and rubber-banded,
which would (all but the dog still sleeping)
over my Brazilian extra-bold unfold only for me."

*

Dmitri's music, as I mentioned, is not easy,
as his life under Stalin was not easy:
celebrated, denounced in *Pravda*, censored,
awarded prizes, threatened, censored,
lionized again. In the siege of Leningrad
(1941), he composed his Seventh.
That winter no dogs barked;
all had been eaten by the starved.

*

But where's the poem gone now?
What happened to the owl?

*

Known as "knocking owls" in Brazil
for their woodpecker-like, percussive
calls. And the owlets are colored like
their parents, in reverse: instead of chocolate, white-
bodied; in place of pale spectacles, Lone-Ranger
eye masks—the way, in a nightmare, danger
starts out by looking safe, or the way
we can mean the opposite of what it is we say.

*

Shostakovich dwelt in sarcasm, or in irony,
the way Dickinson dwelt (so she wrote) "in Possibility."
Impossible from the start to keep his position fixed.
Was he Communist or anti-Communist?
Was he celebratory or subversive
when quoting Wagner in his *wunderkind* First?

*

Easier to read a poem with a heron rising
from a green morning pond, like the spirit rising...

*

This one, patched together,
wants to praise disturbing beauty.

The Great Horned Owl
(Bubo virginianus)

also known as the Tiger Owl,
consumes almost everything
within its vast range:

rabbit, rat, weasel,
squirrel and mouse, vole;
reptiles, fish, amphibians,
crustaceans, all bird life
(including other owls)—
small prey killed instantly,
gripped in curved talons,
and most swallowed whole,

as Grendel in *Beowulf* gulped
men in the mead-hall,
"*fet ond folma*,"
feet and hands.

But this is no monster,
and those are not horns—
in sunlight, barred breast
glinting, ear-tuft feathers
breeze-waved,

like some Book-of-Hours
gallant, on gilt page un-aging,
in gay hunting hat.

And aren't we thrilled when
a bird can seize a mammal
three to four times its size:
skunk, porcupine—even
the occasional small dog?

Who'd censure a splendor—
owl or artist with ambition
to take it all in?

Mobbed by crows, working solo,
incapable of un-candor.

Blakiston's Fish Owl
(Bubo blakistoni)

The world's largest owl, and probably the most endangered—
although the Ainu of Hokkaido
(where there remain one, maybe two hundred birds)
revere it as "God-that-Protects-the-Village"
and break holes in winter river ice,
stocking them each night with fish.

In Russia, several hundred more, steadily less:
trapped in snares set for fur-bearing mammals,
drowned in salmon nets. The portly owls,
for food (or superstition's sake), shot.

Googling, I found:

Thomas Wright Blakiston—Son of a second Baronet, Victorian naturalist and explorer, who, after strenuous expeditions in Canada, China, Japan, died at 58 of pneumonia in the state of Ohio and was buried in the Green Lawn Cemetery (just blocks, as it happens, from where we lived for two decades when I taught in that state).

Henry Seebohm—English steel manufacturer, ornithologist and traveler, who named the bird after Thomas Wright Blakiston, *Bubo blakistoni*. The Grey Emu-tail bird, the *Dromaeocercus seebohmi*, in turn was named after him.

William Tuke—Quaker Grandfather of Henry Seebohm's mother, Esther Wheeler. Horrified by the death of Hannah Mills under appalling conditions in the York Lunatic Asylum, he founded The Retreat (still extant), an institution for what became known as "moral treatment" of the mentally ill. Tuke's was a lonely voice opposing the East India Company for its inhumane impact on other countries. His enterprising mother, Mary, started the tea business, which, after the Second World War, became known as Twinings.

Everything is connected to everything.

Other reasons the Blakiston's is disappearing:
depredation of riparian forests;
small clutch size (sometimes only a single egg);
human over-fishing; power lines and cars.

The extinction of this fish owl (more properly an eagle owl)
is not a metaphor for our own lives' losses—
although of course we will think of them,
the way our species can never not think of itself.

Catch the Blakiston's on YouTube as it catches
a small fish (talons first, gelid water):

soon, one more thing that was once here,
something competent and clear-eyed as that.

The Eastern Screech Owl
(Megascops asio)

Whinnies and low, hooing trills,
brief barks or catlike mews.

These birds don't really screech or scream,
unless it's silently—

like a wife who doesn't know
whether to stay, or go.

The Long-Whiskered Owlet
(Xenoglaux loweryi)

If "Hope is the thing with feathers,"
what could be more hopeful
than this minute Peruvian owl:
superadded feathers

worn as a kind of half-mask (the
Carnival-of-Venice
Columbina)—lacy plumes framing
eyes of somber amber?

What hope, though, for the bird, whose name
means strange? In cloud-forest
disappearing, it's disappearing—
short-tailed and stubby-winged,

five inches high, human-heart sized.
Strange—even in the old,
hope beats with the same strong beat: to taste
something else, to see more,

to do what you once thought you might,
and to wake where you're loved.

The Snowy Owl
(Bubo scandiacus)

You are thinking of the male,
almost purely white.
The larger female's flecked with black.

Are his ideas abstract,
hers not so strict?

He heard, rather than saw, the hare
—no-color on no-color fear—
then talons, beak, and red.

She warms her clutch
of round eggs on the ground.
The chicks hatch gray to blend
with summer tundra; the young
are barred with black.

And here, in my first draft,
I rushed to say, "He thinks
in terms of white and red—
the more iconic, striking mate;
her thoughts run to mottled,
streaked, love-blotched."

But some male birds
come heavily black-flecked;
some feed their young.
And females also hunt.

First thought, *not* best.
Where else might this owl lead?

Never suppose you know another mind.

When hunting, be alone, and camouflaged.

Whether or not you see the marks, all love is maculate.

Hume's Tawny Owl
(Strix butleri)

Near floodlights attracting moths,
it feeds beside the Dead Sea—
a pale bird made paler
by artificial glare. Flitting,
silent, in evening air,
it must look (I haven't been there)
like a giant moth,
hawking the normal-sized.

An owl as flying insect.

A flightless human as. . .

The Barred Owl
(Strix varia)

Old, I am like the barred owl
who has carried voles all night
to the screeching nest, assiduous,
and who, in damp, first light
rests, fluffed and blinking, on a branch.

Because my twenties corresponded
with French New Wave Cinema,
and the bird has dark, soulful eyes
(and because of that word "barred"),

I think of Jean-Paul Belmondo
in his moody roles as street-tough,
no one's idea of a steady, family man!

Here we sit, solitary—unsmiling,
but not without quiet pleasure:
the actor, the owl; the old woman myself.

Smoking a *Gauloise* in the rain.

About the Author

Jeredith Merrin is the author of *Cup*, a special selection by X.J. Kennedy for the Able Muse Book Award, and two books that appeared in the University of Chicago Press Phoenix Poets series: *Shift* and *Bat Ode*. In addition, she has published a book of literary criticism: *An Enabling Humility: Marianne Moore, Elizabeth Bishop, and the Uses of Tradition*. Her poems have appeared in a variety of journals, including *Ploughshares, Slate, Southern Poetry Review, Virginia Quarterly Review,* and *The Yale Review*.

Notes and References

I refer the reader to www.owlpages.com. This site has owl photos (including all birds that appear in this chapbook), species lists, and owl sounds.

p. 22: *The owl, for all his feathers, was a-cold* is a quotation from John Keats' "The Eve of St. Agnes."

p. 25: For the Dmitri Shostakovich photograph alluded to in "The Spectacled Owl," see: https://en.wikipedia.org/wiki/Dmitri_Shostakovich. Darwin's first day in Brazil (February 29, 1832) was recorded in *The Journal of Researches* (1839), reissued as *The Voyage of the Beagle*. This poem employs vowel rhyme and also parodies (in separate, short passages) two well-known contemporary poets.

The following books and websites assisted this work:

Backhouse, Frances. *Owls of North America*. Buffalo: Firefly Books, 2008.

Hume, Rob. *Owls of the World* (Illustrated by Trevor Boyer). Philadelphia: Running Press, 1991.

Johnsgard, Paula. *North American Owls* (second edition). Washington: Smithsonian Institution Press, 2002.

Mikkola, Heimo. *Owls of the World, a Photographic Guide*. Buffalo: Firefly Books, 2012.

O'Brien, Stacey. *Wesley the Owl: The Remarkable Story of an Owl and his Girl*. Washington: Free Press (Simon & Schuster), 2008.

Taylor, Marianne. *Owls*. Ithaca: Comstock Publishing Associates, a division of Cornell University, 2012.